# The Act is Up

Rahmah Ibrahim

The Act is Up © 2022 Rahmah Ibrahim

All rights reserved.

No part of this publication may be reproduced, stored in a retrieval system, or transmitted, in any form or by any means, electronic, mechanical, photocopying, recording or otherwise, without the prior written permission of the presenters.

Rahmah Ibrahim asserts the moral right to be identified as author of this work.

Presentation by *BookLeaf Publishing*

Web: www.bookleafpub.com

E-mail: info@bookleafpub.com

ISBN: 9789357695817

First edition 2022

*I dedicate this piece to Her.*

# ACKNOWLEDGEMENT

I want to thank God, myself, my family, my friends and my very few crushes.

# PREFACE

Pause, have a seat, grab a cup of coffee or tea, and read aloud emotions of a youthful girl coming to terms with the realness of life and love.

# Lift me up

Lift me up,

Don't just accept me as weak

In all the chaos that I am, I am strong for you.

For me, however? My strength has never been
capable of holding me, carrying me, supporting
me

In its very design, it was made for those I love.

So, I ask you again, can you lift me up?

# Why I am scared to trust

Can I trust that you'll keep me safe?

That the insides no one else has had the

privilege of seeing, feeling, or touching lay bare
for you to do as you please.

With the key I unknowingly gave you, what are
your plans for me?

…we have established that I will fight fires for
you, even as they engulf me.

We both know I will somehow come out
unscathed. I do.

But in my vulnerability and openness with you,
lies the opportunity to destroy me to dust…

in that alone is why I am scared to trust.

Yet, I give that decision to you too,

can I trust you?

# Dear me

Dear me,

How you beautify everything is a mystery.

How you love everything is a confusion,

given your history…

I truly am left without speech,

How you shine on everything you accompany, in
spite of your plight, amazes me.

How? How? How?

How do you give so much of yourself, yet
there's no direct supply to you.

You confuse me, I love you, and I trust you more
than I can even understand.

Somehow, you do it.

# Reason and logic

In energy we recline, we rise, we haste.

We live, we cry, we can taste.

There's a part of our experiences that is not
made for words but just for feeling.

 Why can't we, in energy embrace the things that
make our heart race?

Do we always have to have reason and logic be
a part of the very moments that are made up of
nothing but energy?

Oh, can't we just inhale deeply this energy and
confront it without the need of words or
translation or explanation? Energy is its own
mediator, explainer, interpreter.

Let breath and let be.

For we really can leave it up to energy, to enjoy
our states.

# Her only fault

She.

A full sentence, a full breath, a fiery heart,

incapable of being incapable, her only fault was

that others were so enraptured by her that

they couldn't see any of them.

She knew though and was so happy to hug every
last flaw that she found in herself and decorated
them all to suit her.

Afterall, what was she if not for herself?

# Always being introduced

I am honored to meet me. Again, and again.

When we finally recognize that we were never known, have never been known and will never be known, we will be able to really live life.

Every moment you are becoming a new you and you are always being introduced to each new face of yourself; I find that beautiful.

So much love and beauty and newness in the oldest stranger to ever exist.

Me.
Within,
        me.

# Sunset of who we are

The sunset of who we are is embarrassingly
absurd.

Emotions, memories, half-crafted ideas of
people, inauthenticity, trouble using our voice
and speaking our minds even as we seek out the
sounds of others locked-in cries and try to be the
shoulder for another.

I can create a record-breaking pastry called "the
most flakey" out of our inabilities.

But really, doesn't our very ability to choose
inactivity, stillness, reserve and self-preservation
give cause for pause.

We can choose chaos and in that very choice lies
perfect beauty.

# Embrace me so fully

Day 8: Poem 8

Of all the Me's I used to be

I miss the one that loved me the hardest, the most.

And in retrospect, those were the versions that caused me to look in the mirror the most,

to hold my own hand,

to catch me as I fell.

I recollect those memories of me and finally start to understand why I embrace me so fully.

I wish I could gift me, to me.

# Carry me

In true catalyst fashion,

I lost myself in finding myself,

 and right now, as I drown and lose sight of the shore…

There's an underlying relief, in finally

…being carried.

# How lucky she is

And she stared at the empty spot where her goals had resided in her chest,

she glanced deep into the recesses of her core to find that her goals had somehow been incinerated and now covered every bit of her being

...she,

who once held firmly onto her ambitions and goals, no longer had hands large enough or arms sturdy enough to encompass this new thriving world of hers.

She was due to start sharing and welcoming new inhabitants, to help her make her world into a home.

Oh, how lucky she is to carry her home within her, to carry a space so full of her own fortune.

How lucky she is.

# Intuition and love

Love,

It creeps up on you, but often it is riddled with intuition.

I can finally breath my own essence without shame, but I knew…

I knew when you were finally seeing the same. I can finally acknowledge my charm and shine but I wish I was made aware from your own mouth and not mine.

I know me and I love me. Through our own love-leave.

How come I never looked in the mirror until I fell in love with someone,

that taught me more about me.

# Bare me and burn me

You are a flame around me,

warming me from a distance but when I get too
close,

burning me in an instant,

How can I survive the winter when you bare me
and burn me all in one breath?

Am I supposed to become Ice to embrace you?

Am I supposed to find armor like everyone else
in this love-leave war?

What if I want to dive in and burn?

 Will you, let you—end me?

# Sanity and satin

Sanity and satin,

Never suited me

Wild and wise always flattered me,

If all I have is my crazy,

Nothing can shatter me

Nothing can shatter me.

# Any of you, at all

If I was given poison right now,

I would drink it to mute the agony of not being near you,

not being able to hear you.

If I could mute these feelings in my chest,
I would,

I fear I have forfeited all good,

And worst of it all is…

I haven't even touched,

kissed

or felt what it feels like to unmask the veil of friendship and admit the boundlessness of my interest in you,

I have intuition, but I also have dignity,

They battle for the forefront.

Somehow, I feel like I have lost everything

without gaining any of you,

Any of you, at all.

# Under my skin

I close my eyes,

And I see your smile,

Enclosing in on me, in a place

No one has ever been.

This is out of my control,

But if there is anyone I'd let under my skin,

And around my inhibitions,

It's,

You.

# A knowing

There's a deep internal acknowledgment of my

significance,

But sadly, this world doesn't spin on knowing,

There's a certain sheen of beauty all over me

when I put on my favorite skirt or do things that

 inspire me,

These things find me glowing…

There is a certain level of comfort in my own

smile coming from something I did for me, then

ever being able to accept a compliment or

Even believe the things you try to show me,

About me

There's a deep, incomparable gratitude in

loving me more than I love you, that keeps me

overflowing and that is how I can fill you up

more than you can understand.

And that is how I remain a standing,

blossoming, blooming flower in a rippling

rainforest made for the thick veiny, viny sorts.

And that is how I remain.

And that is how I will maintain,

me.

# You are,

You are,

in every single fiber of your being, wholly capable.

You are,

In every shyness-turned-determined stage, insanely able.

You are,

In every attempt, failure and win, undeniably irreplaceable.

You are,

In every self-deprecating thought, lesson learned, and smile found, blindingly beautiful.

I thought you should know…

You are, more than this world thought it could handle.

And now that you're here, you take it by storm.

You.

Win.

# Claw my way back

I love getting older,

I have more strength in my shoulders,

I hug myself and find my roots…

And claw my way back to my youth, to find

explanations within my new inspirations for

why I have done what I have done.

For how I have become 'the one'',

In searching for 'the one'.

I must have missed the memo,

that all this time she was dressed in yellow,

waiting, loving and smiling at me from my own
mirror.

It is—Indeed—very funny, how all along she

was right in front of me.

# Beneath which rivers flow

Heaven is a faraway place,

This fact does not make it any less of a reality,

any less elusive to me,

I feel deep in myself that I have all the

hardware to get me to hell,

I claw, I cry, I work hard,

I try,

But somehow, I default into the fear of never

being worthy of the place beneath which rivers
flow.

I know, I am directed, guided and instructed

but my very being writhes free and does her own
thing.

How can I convince her?

How can I get her on my side?

I need her to claw, to cry, to work hard,

To try,

To somehow lose fault and want what I want.

Otherwise, we will be split up.

After.

And who knows which hereafter we'll earn.

We're going to learn.

# Unlike any other

I peek, I get bold, I say I want this, I say I don't
need that,

Then a moment comes, unlike any other where

something happens that alters me.

Again, I am in circles peeking all the same,

aspiring, feeling left behind, struggling to be

outstanding but just standing out.

Separating myself, being happy and then in

retrospect confused why I let it happen.

Why must I confuse myself, and at the same

time have no control of myself?

I want agency over me, my finances, my life

and my choices; but I fear I won't recognize

me, when I give me the key.

The real me.

For she hides…nothing: she's bold, she's

messy, she's aspiring,

 she's aiming, she's cunning, she's beautiful,

she's unrestricted, she's feeling, she's hard,

she's soft, she's a creative, she's a philosopher,

 she's a healer, she's open, she's pure,

she's peace, she's calm, she's a storm,

she's dark, she's hurt, she's fixed,

she's whole, she's satisfied, she's grasping,

She… is the real me,

I just have her shielded for her own protection,

Like I am shielded for my own collection.

One day, we might collide, and I fear that day

more than I know how to describe.

# Filter

There's a certain loss that happens when you

filter all your thoughts, expressions and

feelings through the lens of your audience,

There must not be a filter,

You are your biggest fan, and your biggest
supporter, mustn't you cater your art, your glitter
and glamour, the angle of the stage- at you?

Should you give a damn what the onlookers
think?

If there needs to be a filter, it needs to be one

that blocks the doorway to your show, filtering

out any restricting person, any negative Nancy,

any envious friend,

That is the only filter you must tolerate,

For your show is about to start and you need to

be fluid, free and engulfed in you,

Now go out there and smile at you, perform for

you, and do you- for you.

www.ingramcontent.com/pod-product-compliance
Lightning Source LLC
LaVergne TN
LVHW010953200726

843509LV00013B/2395